This Book Belongs to

Courtney Marie Hall
Love, Aunty Marie

# Tell me about
# Jesus

By MARY ALICE JONES
Illustrated by DOROTHY GRIDER

RAND M<sup>C</sup>NALLY & COMPANY

## BIBLE REFERENCES (*in order of the reference in the text*)

| | | |
|---|---|---|
| Matthew 2:1 | Matthew 15:39 | Matthew 23:13-14 |
| Luke 2:52 | Luke 13:10-13 | John 9 |
| Matthew 13:3-9 | Luke 2:8-14 | Luke 13:10-17 |
| Matthew 13:33 | Luke 15:3-6 | Matthew 13:54-57a |
| John 10:1-10 | Luke 19:1-9 | Luke 15:1-2 |
| Luke 18:10-14 | Matthew 25:34-40 | Luke 23:2 |
| Matthew 18:12-13 | Luke 9:51-56 | John 5:9-18 |
| Matthew 6:1-4 | Luke 19:45 | John 15:15-17 |
| Matthew 7:24-27 | Matthew 23 | Matthew 21:45 |
| Luke 9:48 | Mark 10:46-52 | John 6:15 |
| Luke 15:9 | John 5:2-9 | John 10:29-33 |
| Matthew 18:14 | Matthew 9:9 | Mark 14:17 to 15:39 |
| Matthew 9:9-13 | Matthew 11:28 | John 7:13 |
| Mark 12:37c | Matthew 19:13-15 | Luke 23:34 |
| Luke 18:10-14 | Mark 5:22-24 | Luke 24:36-50 |
| Matthew 6:26, 28-29 | Matthew 19:16-22 | Matthew 28:16-20 |
| Luke 10:38, 39 | Luke 12:15-34 | John 20:19-21 |
| Luke 7:36 | Luke 10:22 | Acts 2:23-24 |
| John 2:1-2 | John 1:14-18 | Acts 2:38-42 |
| Luke 5:1-6 | John 3:34-35 | Acts 4 |
| Matthew 13:1-2 | Matthew 5:20 | Acts 5:17-42 |

*Library of Congress Catalog Card Number: 67-18282*

ISBN 528-87657-0

Second Paperback Printing, 1977

# Contents

# Where Jesus Lived

BOBBY and his daddy and mother and his little sister Mary were in New York on a vacation. They had looked in the gay windows of the stores along the busy streets and ridden on the subway and had a drive in Central Park and gone to the children's museum. Now they were high in a tall building, looking out of a window over the city to the sea beyond it.

"Look, Daddy," Bobby called. "See those ships? Are they going to cross the ocean?"

"Some of them are, I am sure, Bobby."

"Can we go to see the ships? Close up, I mean?"

Daddy looked at Mother and she nodded. "I think that would be fine, don't you, Mary? If a ship is sailing today, maybe we can go on board and pretend we are going to cross the ocean."

Mary didn't understand much about it but she wanted to go.

Daddy looked in the newspaper. "A ship is sailing today," he reported. "It is open to visitors right now."

So they took a taxi to the pier where the big ship was being loaded. It was a busy place! Crowds were hurrying, travelers with tickets in their hands, friends coming to see them off. Porters were moving baggage and messengers were bringing flowers.

Daddy took Bobby's hand and Mother took Mary's hand and they went up the visitors' gangplank into the ship.

They saw the outside decks like big covered porches where people were walking. Inside, they saw the big dining room, the living room, the children's playroom and the tidy little bedrooms—the places where passengers would live during the trip.

"Let's stay on the ship and go with it," Bobby teased.

"Maybe someday you can really go," Daddy replied. "Right now we shall pretend we are sailing with the ship."

"Where is it going, Daddy?"

"Across the ocean, then all the way through the Mediterranean Sea to Haifa." Daddy pointed to a big map on the wall and showed Bobby where the ship would travel.

"It is going a long way," Bobby said.

Daddy nodded. "And into an interesting part of the world."

Then a gong sounded and a call came out of the loudspeaker. "All visitors ashore!" Daddy and Mother and Bobby and Mary went down the gangplank. From the shore they watched and waved while confetti was thrown, and the tugboats pushed, and the ship began to move away, out toward the ocean.

When they were back at their hotel, Bobby was thinking about the ship. "You said it was going to an interesting part of the world, Daddy. What is interesting about it?"

"Many things are happening in that part of the world today, Bobby. But we are especially interested in it because it is the part of the world where Jesus lived."

Bobby looked surprised. "You mean that ship is going to where Jesus lived?"

"To the same part of the world." Daddy saw Bobby's puzzled face. "Jesus lived in a real place, you know."

Mother was brushing Mary's hair. "Does it seem strange, Bobby, that ships and airplanes go there today?"

"I hadn't thought about it like that." Bobby grinned. "I guess I thought it was just something in the Bible."

Mother put a ribbon on Mary's hair. "The Bible does tell

us about it. But what it tells us about is something real. Jesus was a real person who lived in a real place."

"Bobby, I have a picture of Jesus," Mary offered. "I will show it to you when we get home."

Daddy smiled. "Your picture of Jesus is the way someone thought he looked, dear. No photographers or painters made pictures of Jesus which show us just how he looked. But we know that Jesus himself was real. And we know where he lived and can go there."

"I am glad we saw that ship," Bobby concluded. "It makes Jesus more real to know travelers can get on a ship and go where he lived."

# How Jesus Grew

JOHN lived next door to Bobby on one side and Susan lived next door on the other side. They were in the same room at school. One afternoon on the way home they saw a nursery-school child break away from his group and dart toward the street.

They raced after the little boy and caught him at the curb. He laughed as if it were a game.

But Susan held him tight. "No," she said firmly, "you cannot go into the street." Then the patrol mother reached them and took the little boy's hand as she held up traffic, and led the children across the street.

On the other side, walking toward their own street, John said crossly, "That little boy should stay where he belongs. He should know better than to run out that way."

Bobby laughed. "That's because you don't have a little sister, John. I know we have to look after Mary."

"And I have Jack," Susan added. "I have to watch him."

"I'm glad I know how to look after myself," John declared.

When they came to their own block they saw Bobby's mother in the yard with Mary and stopped to tell about the little boy.

"I wouldn't run into the street," Mary announced.

"I am sure you wouldn't, dear," Mother agreed. "You are growing up and learning fast how to look after yourself."

"But Jack isn't big enough yet," Susan said. "I always have to hold his hand on the sidewalk."

Bobby flopped down on the ground. "Growing is interesting. Jack doesn't understand at all. Mary is just beginning to understand. Susan and John and I are big enough to know all about traffic rules and why we must obey them."

"But even you have a lot of growing yet to do," Mother reminded him.

"And a lot of learning, too," Susan added. "The sixth grade knows more than we do about lots of things."

"Does everybody have to take so much time to grow and learn?" John asked. "Like that little boy. And Jack. I think it takes too long. Why can't people do it quicker?"

Mother laughed. "Well, John, mothers and daddies sometimes wonder about that, too. Why their children don't learn quicker. But it seems that growing and learning do take time."

Bobby looked thoughtful. "I was wondering, Mother. Did Jesus grow and learn, too? Like we do?"

"I think he did, Bobby. He was once a baby like Mrs. Miller's baby in the next block. Then he was a little boy like Jack. Then he was a big boy like you. Then he was a man."

"Did he have to learn everything? Like not to run into the street?" Susan asked.

Mother smiled. "I do not know about that, Susan. He lived in a little town before there were automobiles. I think learning not to run into the streets was not as important for him as it is for Jack."

"But he did have to learn? About reading, and rules for games, and working?" John persisted.

"We do not know all about how Jesus grew," Mother answered. "The Bible doesn't tell us what he did year after year. It says he grew 'in wisdom and stature and in favor with God and man.' "

"I wish it had told us more," Bobby said. "I would like to know all about him when he was a boy like me."

"Why did he have to grow and learn?" Susan inquired. "He was different. Why couldn't he know everything all at once?"

"Nobody knows just how to answer that question, Susan. But I think it was so we could know he understood how it feels to be a child and how people learn day by day what they are to be and to do. Jesus showed us God is with us as we grow."

Mother turned to Bobby and measured his height with her hands. "I think when Jesus was about your age he was about your size. And maybe he wondered why some of the words in the books at his school were so hard to pronounce, just as you do."

"But Jesus didn't have to learn to think about other people as we do, did he?" Bobby asked. "Even when he was a boy? He was always good, wasn't he?"

"Not just automatically good, I think, son. The Bible tells us about times when Jesus had to decide what was right."

"Then I think he knew it was hard sometimes," John said.

"I like to think about Jesus growing and learning," Bobby decided. "I am glad he understood how it is to be a boy."

# Everyday Things Were Important to Jesus

THE librarian had suggested a book to Bobby. It was about people who had done something important to help their country. He and his daddy had been reading it together at home. Now Bobby walked around the room.

"Daddy, I'm glad these men did all those great things, but it makes me feel bad, too."

Daddy looked up. "Why does it make you feel bad, son?"

"Because I can't ever do things like that. They are too big. I will never know enough or be good enough."

"I am not sure about that," Daddy countered. "You have a lot of time to grow and learn, you know."

Bobby stood still and stared at Daddy. "Do you mean some-day boys may be reading about something big I have done?"

Daddy chuckled. "Well, I am not promising that, son. Not many people get written up in books." He was serious again. "But what ordinary people do is important, too. Remember how often Jesus talked about people who did the ordinary things?"

"Tell me about them, Daddy."

"Once Jesus told a story about a farmer who sowed seed; another time about a shepherd who looked after his sheep. He talked about a woman who made bread for her family, and about men working in the fields and building houses."

Bobby nodded. He remembered these stories. Daddy went on. "Jesus himself worked in a carpenter shop. He understood about the everyday things people had to do. He knew most people would never do anything other people would call great."

"But why did Jesus talk so much about such ordinary people doing such ordinary things?" Bobby wanted to know.

"Jesus lived among these people, son."

"You mean they were his friends? He liked them?"

18

"Jesus was with them day after day. To him, these people and their everyday work really counted for something. He wanted to help them understand they were important to God."

Bobby picked up his book. "There are a few famous people like these men," he said. "But I guess there are always more ordinary people like me."

"Because Jesus knew ordinary people were important, he disturbed other teachers around him," Daddy explained.

"How did he disturb them?" Bobby asked.

"They thought God cared most about people who kept all the rules of proper behavior and people who held important positions. But Jesus showed people that God cared about little children and people who had done wrong and people who had to work hard to feed their families and people the others despised."

"I think the ordinary people would be glad about that."

"Yes, they were, son. The Bible says that the great throng heard him gladly."

Bobby sat down by his daddy and opened his book. "Let's read some more. We need some great men. But I'm glad Jesus showed the people ordinary ones are important, too."

# Being Glad in God's World

BOBBY and John and Susan had gone by bus on an out-of-town field trip with their class. They visited a large farm where there were many fine horses.

"Look at that man combing the horse's coat," Susan called. "Why is he doing that?"

"Suppose you ask him," their teacher suggested.

The man seemed surprised at the question. "We want to keep his coat clean and healthy," he told them. "Horses get burrs and dirt in their coats. Brushing makes the coats shine." He smiled at Susan. "It is something like the way your mother wants you to brush your hair to keep it shiny."

They saw colts with their mothers and men teaching horses to wear saddles and men teaching horses to trot.

There were other horses which had been used as riding horses for a long time. These were saddled for the boys and girls who wanted to see how it felt to ride. They were helped into the saddles and men led the horses around the farm.

Bobby spoke to the man leading his horse. "Can I hold the reins myself?" he asked. "While you walk by the horse?"

"Let's see how you get along," the man answered. He put the reins into Bobby's hands and showed him how to hold them.

"This is more fun than riding in a car," Bobby called.

John called back, "But not so fast."

The boys and girls had a fine time taking turns. They squealed and felt important sitting in the saddles.

When it was time for them to leave, they thanked the men who had shown them the horses and let them ride. Back at school they told their teacher good-bye and started toward home.

"I like horses," John declared.

"I had never been on one before and I was afraid at first," Susan admitted. "But then I liked it. And I loved the colts and the horses' shiny coats."

After dinner that night Bobby told his mother and daddy about the good time they had had. "We ought to go on more field trips," he declared. "We have fun and get to know each other better and do something new."

Daddy nodded. "Having friends and doing new things make life pleasant and interesting."

After a moment Bobby went on. "I have been wondering, Daddy. Did Jesus have any good times? Like we had today?"

"I am sure he did, son. What are you thinking of?"

"He was so busy. So many people needed him. When did he have time for any fun?"

"The Bible tells us about his visiting in peoples' homes and enjoying flowers and birds," Daddy began. "And going to parties and riding in a boat on the lake."

"Jesus liked children," Mary reminded Bobby. "I think he had a good time with them because they loved him."

"I think he did too, dear." Mother turned to Bobby. "I think Jesus did not make the difference between having a good time and helping people that we sometimes make."

"But, Mother, he couldn't have a good time helping sick people and lonely people all the time," Bobby protested.

"Maybe not a good time in the sense of laughing and shouting the way you did when you saw the clowns at the fair last month. Or when you were riding the horses this afternoon. But Jesus *liked* helping people, Bobby."

Daddy agreed. "I think Jesus felt joyous and happy as he helped a suffering woman stop hurting and a lame man walk."

"Was Jesus really happy, Daddy?"

"He often did not have an easy time, Bobby. But having an easy time is not the same as being joyous and happy."

"Isn't it, Daddy?"

"You remember the Christmas story, son. The angels who announced the birth of Jesus to the shepherds said they were bringing good news. 'Good news of a great joy which will come to all the people,' is the way the Bible puts it."

"What does it mean, Daddy? That Jesus was good news?"

"I think that is the way it is, Bobby. Jesus was good news from God and good news about God. That God cares about people! So Jesus himself was joyous even when life was hard."

Mother folded the sweater she had been knitting. "Many of the stories Jesus told were about people being glad. The shepherd who found his lost lamb called in neighbors to rejoice with him. And the father whose son came back home had a party to tell the good news. He said to his friends, 'Rejoice with me.' "

"I guess it does make a person happy to tell good news," Bobby remembered. "Like the time Susan's grandmother was so sick. When I told you the doctor said she was going to be all right, it was good news for you. I was glad to tell you."

"Maybe that helps you understand, Bobby," Daddy said. "Jesus' whole life was good news. He showed men life is meant to be good because God is good. He showed us how to find joy in our world." Daddy roughed Bobby's hair. "Whether we are riding horses or helping sick people or working hard."

# Jesus Helped People Change

BOBBY was feeling grumbly. "Henry doesn't play fair," he told his daddy as they were bringing in some wood for the fireplace. "And he is mean to dogs. He kicked Samson and threw a rock at Rover. Nobody likes him."

"Not playing fair and being mean to dogs are bad ways of behaving," Daddy agreed. "They upset other people. I wonder why Henry behaves that way."

Bobby looked puzzled. "How can I know why he does it, Daddy? I guess he just likes to be mean."

"Maybe so. But I wonder, Bobby. Do you think having a friend might help him?"

"But why should I help him?" Bobby complained. "*I* don't like him either. I don't want to be friends with him."

"People often feel that way about those who upset them," Daddy said. "Some friends of Jesus felt that way about a man Jesus met."

"Tell me about it, Daddy."

"Zacchaeus was a tax collector for Rome, the nation that had conquered the country where Jesus lived. The people hated having Roman soldiers in their country. Even more they despised their own countrymen who collected taxes to pay the Romans."

"I see why people didn't like Zacchaeus," Bobby said.

"They would not go to see him or invite him to their houses. They even looked the other way when he passed by," Daddy continued. "The people thought he cheated, too. That he took more money than the Romans required and kept it for himself."

"How did a man like that meet Jesus?" Bobby asked.

"In a strange way, son." Daddy smiled. "Even a funny way."

"Go on, Daddy."

"Zacchaeus had heard about Jesus. When he came to Jericho, Zacchaeus' city, there was a big crowd. Zacchaeus wanted very much to see Jesus, but the tax collector was too short to see over the people. So he ran ahead and climbed a tree."

Bobby laughed. "That was funny. A man in a tree."

Daddy nodded. "Because the people did not like him anyway, they made fun of him. But when Jesus looked up and saw Zacchaeus, he did not laugh. Instead, his face was friendly."

"But didn't Jesus know Zacchaeus was bad?" Bobby asked.

"I am sure Jesus knew about Zacchaeus, Bobby. But Jesus understood what the others did not understand. He understood that Zacchaeus was unhappy and lonely."

"What did Jesus do about it?"

"He surprised everybody, son. Zacchaeus most of all."

"How did he, Daddy?"

"Though Zacchaeus had one of the finest houses in town, nobody had visited him for a long time. Now Jesus called, 'Zacchaeus, I would like to stay at your house.' Zacchaeus looked startled, then pleased. He climbed down and hurried to his own gate. When Jesus came, Zacchaeus received him joyously."

"But why did Jesus want to visit a man like that?"

"That is what Jesus' friends asked, son. They grumbled,

'Jesus has gone to visit a sinner.' But Jesus understood that Zacchaeus needed him even more than the other people did."

"What happened at Zacchaeus' house, Daddy?"

"Something very interesting happened. Jesus did not accuse Zacchaeus of cheating. Instead, Zacchaeus spoke of it. 'I will pay back to every man I have cheated,' he said. 'Yes, I will pay back four times as much as I have taken unfairly.'"

Bobby grinned. "He paid a lot for his cheating."

"That was not all," Daddy went on. "Looking at Jesus, Zacchaeus suddenly knew that he was on the wrong track. He did not want to go on being a selfish man piling up money for himself. He wanted to help people, to be friendly. He said to

Jesus, 'I will give half of all the money I have to help the poor.' "

"Did Zacchaeus really change, Daddy? Did he stop cheating people and start being good to them?"

"I think he did, son."

"Did he change just because Jesus came to see him?"

"I think it was because Jesus showed Zacchaeus he cared about him. That even a tax collector for the Romans who had cheated was important to God."

"I guess that would make a difference," Bobby agreed. "After everybody had hated him, to have Jesus care about him. Care enough to help him change."

"Not just change the way he acted, son. Jesus helped Zacchaeus to feel different inside. To change his idea of the person he wanted to be and of what was important to him."

Bobby remembered Henry who cheated and hurt dogs. "Zacchaeus changed because Jesus cared about him. But I am not like Jesus. Even if I were friends with Henry, that would not help anything."

"Maybe not, Bobby. We do not understand another person as Jesus did. We cannot be *sure* what will help. But how about trying the way of showing Henry somebody cares about him?"

"How can I, Daddy? What can I do to show him?"

"Suppose you and I ask Henry to go with us tomorrow to the high-school basketball game?"

Bobby was not sure he wanted to but he agreed to try it. So Bobby and Henry and Daddy saw an exciting game.

"I had a good time today," Henry said when they stopped to let him out at his house.

As they drove on, Bobby looked at Daddy. "You know, Henry was different, too! We had fun together. I'm glad we asked him to go with us." He thought a minute. "It's good you knew about Jesus and Zacchaeus, Daddy. It gave us a good new idea."

"Remembering Jesus often gives us good new ideas, Bobby."

# Celebrating Christmas

THE boys and girls at Bobby's church were planning for Christmas. They learned the songs for the Christmas Eve family service and planned their own part in the service.

As they walked home after the meeting, Susan was thoughtful. "Christmas is Jesus' birthday, but we give other people presents. I'd like to give Jesus a birthday present."

John looked puzzled. "How can we give Jesus presents?"

They had reached their own street. "Let's ask Mother about it," Bobby suggested. "I think she understands it."

Mother and Mary waved from the window. While the others were hanging up their coats and telling about the program, Mother poured hot chocolate she had made and Mary brought cookies. They sat on the floor around the fireplace.

"Mother, we have been wondering," Bobby began. "Is there any way we can give Jesus a birthday present?"

"We sing songs and have stories," Mary said.

"Yes, Mary," Bobby responded. "But that's to *remember* his

33

birthday. We would like to give him a real present.''

"What do you think he would like, Bobby?'' Mother asked.

Bobby thought a moment. "We decided what Jesus wanted most was for people to feel God's love and to love each other.''

"Doesn't that help you answer your question, son? About how we can honor Jesus on his birthday?''

"You mean by helping other people to know God's love? And to love each other?'' Bobby asked. "But how can we do that?''

"One way you have been planning at church. A service to remind people Jesus came to show them God loves them.''

"I think that is a nice way,'' Mary said.

Bobby finished his hot chocolate and put down his cup. "But I think we should do more than that.''

Susan agreed. "We can show love to people ourselves.''

"Like giving people Christmas presents?" John asked.

Mother placed the empty cups on the tray. "Not just giving them presents, John. But I think really to show love to someone who needs it is the best way to celebrate Jesus' birthday."

"Tell us more about it, Mother."

"One time when Jesus was talking with his friends, he told them they were blessed whenever they helped sick people or hungry people or lonely people or people who had done wrong. Then he said, 'Truly, I say to you, as you did it to one of the least of these my brethren, you did it to me.'"

Susan nodded slowly. "But there are so many people who need something. People we don't even know about. How can we help all of them?"

"We can't help all of them by ourselves, Susan. Being a part of our church gives us a way to work with many people who

know how to find those who need us and how to help them."

"We heard about some church plans," Bobby remembered.

Mother went on. "In our neighborhood there are lonely people. They give us our own special opportunity to show love."

John looked doubtful. "You mean like old Mr. Jackson? He lives by himself. I guess he is lonely. But he is cross and doesn't like us even to play in front of his house."

"Maybe so, John. But we were talking about *our* showing love to *him*, not *his* showing love to *us*," Mother reminded them.

"It's more fun to do things for people who love us," Bobby protested. "Like our friends and you and Daddy and Mary."

He thought it over. "But that isn't all Jesus meant about showing love, is it? Just doing what is fun?"

Mother smiled. "Not just for fun the way you mean, Bobby.

But if you try showing love the way you think Jesus meant, maybe you will find you will like it."

Susan had an idea. "I know what we can do. We can make Mr. Jackson a Christmas wreath for his door. Like the one we made for the minister at church. I think it would cheer him up."

"That's good, Susan," Bobby said, and they all agreed.

John jumped up. "Let's begin right now. He should have it early so he can begin to feel Christmas in his bones."

So they put on their outdoor things and went to the woods and gathered some sprigs of pine and some cones and pods. The

next day in Bobby's basement they gilded the cones and silvered the pods. They made a wire frame. When they had finished the wreath, Mother helped them make a red bow for the top.

Bobby and Susan and John took the wreath to Mr. Jackson's house. They were a little uneasy as they rang the bell and waited at the door. The old man seemed surprised to see them. He just said, "Thank you," and took the wreath inside. They felt rather let down as they walked away.

The next day they saw the wreath on Mr. Jackson's door. "It looks pretty, whether he likes it or not," Susan said.

Just then the door opened. "Doesn't the wreath make the house look like Christmas?" Mr. Jackson called. "It makes me feel like Christmas inside, too. For the first time in many years."

When he got home, Bobby told his mother about it. "You were right, Mother. Mr. Jackson needed someone to pay attention to him. It was a good way to give Jesus a birthday present."

Mary gave a gay little hop. "I'll go to see Mr. Jackson on Christmas and show him my new doll."

Bobby teased, "You seem sure you will get a doll, Mary."

But Mother gave the little girl a hug. "I know Mr. Jackson will love seeing you and your new doll, dear."

"And I'll bring him home with me to see our tree."

"That will be good, Mary," Mother agreed. "And maybe thinking of honoring Jesus on his birthday will help us remember all year to be good neighbors to Mr. Jackson."

# Being Angry at the Right Time

BOBBY came home from school feeling angry. "Ted and Ralph pushed me out of line in the lunchroom," he told his mother. "I pushed back, but there were two of them."

He threw his books on the table. "Tomorrow I'm going to get John and push them out of line," he blustered.

"Right now let's go to the kitchen and eat an apple and popcorn," Mother suggested. "I think you are hungry."

Bobby finished eating. "I was hungry," he said. "But, Mother, why did Ted and Ralph push me? They shouldn't have done it."

"No, they shouldn't, Bobby." Mother smiled at him. "Ted and Ralph probably were just feeling as if they wanted to show they *could* push someone. They didn't hurt you, did they?"

"No," Bobby admitted. "But it made me mad."

"Nobody likes to be pushed," Mother agreed. She looked at him and laughed. "But most boys *I* know like to push once in a while."

Bobby grinned. "I pushed John yesterday. But it was for fun. Why did it make me so mad today, Mother?"

"I wondered about that. It wasn't serious."

Bobby thought a minute. "Did Jesus ever get angry?"

"Not for the reason you did, son. He didn't think first of how other people treated him but of what was the best way to treat other people. He understood people better than we do."

"I am not like that."

"Neither am I, Bobby. The close friends of Jesus were not like that. They became angry with unfriendly people."

"Tell me about it, Mother."

"One time Jesus and his friends were going to Jerusalem. They were walking. Along the way, messengers were sent ahead to the next town to arrange for a place to stay overnight.

"When Jesus and his friends came near the town, the mes-

sengers met them. 'The people won't let us stay in the town,' they reported. 'They are Samaritans and hate the people of Jerusalem. No one going to Jerusalem can stay in their town.'

"The friends of Jesus were furious. 'It is wicked to mistreat strangers,' they shouted. 'The people should be punished. Let us ask God to send fire to burn down the whole town.' "

"They were really mad," Bobby said. "What did Jesus do?"

"He spoke quietly to his angry friends. 'Would burning down their town make the people feel friendly toward us?' he asked. 'Or get us a place to sleep? Come, let us go to another town.' "

Bobby thought about it. "Those friends were like me. When they were angry they wanted to hurt somebody. But Jesus was right. Burning down towns and pushing people around are not good ways to make men feel friendly."

He thought some more.

"Did Jesus *ever* get angry, Mother?"

"When he saw people being hurt or treated unfairly, Jesus spoke vigorously against the ones who were doing it. Especially when someone who thought he was important was hurting someone who could not stand up for himself."

"Who were the people Jesus spoke against?" Bobby asked.

"Some merchants who had booths in the Temple Court were cheating people who had to buy from them. Jesus strode into their booths and overturned their tables. 'You have made this place a den of robbers!' he accused the merchants."

"Jesus would be angry with men who cheated people who depended on them," Bobby said. "Were there some other times?"

Mother continued. "Some religious leaders were praying out loud in a place where they could be heard by the people. Jesus knew the way they lived. 'You make long prayers and observe the ceremonies,' he said, 'but you are not generous and kind toward other people. You preach but do not practice.' "

Bobby thought about what his mother had told him. "I see what you mean, Mother. Jesus was angry at the right time."

"Jesus knew what was important for men, Bobby. Anything that separated them from God's love and from one another, he opposed vigorously. Whatever it was and whoever did it."

# Jesus Was Close to People

BOBBY and Susan and John had been skating. Suddenly, as they were walking home, a heavy truck out of control came careening down the street straight toward them. Trying to get out of the way, Susan and John ran one way; Bobby ran the other. The truck hit the sidewalk where Bobby was. Susan and John saw the driver's frightened face as they screamed.

The next thing Bobby knew he was in the hospital, bandaged up and hurting all over. He remembered what had happened. He was frightened again. Then he saw his daddy standing close by his bed. Daddy held Bobby's hand tight. Bobby felt better.

Two weeks later Bobby was back home, still bandaged in places, but getting well. Mother and Mary were looking after him. John and Susan had come to see him and told him what the driver of the truck had reported about the brakes failing on the hill and how terrified he had been. The room at school had sent him some cards they had made and all the neighbors had sent him good things to eat. So Bobby was feeling well looked after.

That evening he and his daddy were talking about what had happened. "I was awfully afraid, Daddy," Bobby admitted. "The truck looked like a mountain coming toward me."

Daddy put his arm around him. "I am sure it did, son. It *was* a very big truck. It would have frightened anybody."

"Even when I woke up in the hospital I was afraid," Bobby continued. "I saw it again."

"But you are fine now," Daddy assured him. "Mother told me the doctor said today that all the bandages can come off next week and you can go back to school."

Bobby was quiet a moment. "You know when I stopped being afraid, Daddy?"

"When was it, son?"

"When I saw you close to me and felt your hand."

"A daddy wants to be close by when his son is hurt."

"It made things different. I still hurt but I wasn't afraid."

"That is the way it is when loving people are close to us, Bobby. It helps us bear things and not be afraid even when we are hurt. This is what Jesus showed us about God's love."

"Tell me more about it, Daddy. I want to understand it."

"Jesus always lived close to people. Not in a faraway palace or behind guarded gates, but in the midst of people."

"Mother told me he cared about ordinary people."

Daddy nodded. "He went where children were playing and where beggars waited and where sick people were. He went to a wedding. He went where men were working and where women were drawing water at the village well—wherever people were."

Bobby recalled what he had learned of Jesus. "He seemed always to be where people needed him."

"He wanted them to feel close to him. When he was speaking to people who had worked long and hard and were tired out, he said, 'Come to me. I will help you feel rested.' When his friends were about to send away children who wanted to see him, Jesus called the children to come to him."

"I am glad Jesus was close to people who needed him."

"Jesus showed people what they had not understood about God. God is not a faraway lawmaker watching people to see that they obey the rules. God's love is close to them, drawing them close to him."

Bobby looked at his daddy. "That is important to know."

# *Jesus Wanted Persons To Be Their Best*

THERE were some colored pictures in a magazine about a very rich man and how he lived. Bobby and Susan and John were looking at them in Bobby's basement.

"Just look at that car!" John exclaimed. "It has everything! And I'll bet it can go a hundred miles an hour!"

Bobby touched another picture. "I like the boat best," he declared. "What fun to flash over the water in that beauty!"

"It would be fun to have a fine car and boat," Susan agreed. "But if I had lots of money I would spend most of it on my house and flowers. Aren't these garden pictures gorgeous?"

"With all that money," John declared, "I'd buy anything I wanted, go anywhere I wanted to, do anything I wanted to do."

Bobby's mother came in as John was speaking. "That sounds exciting, doesn't it?"

"It *would* be exciting, Mother," Bobby said, "Not just seem exciting. And it would be fun. More fun than anything."

Mother's eyes twinkled. "How do you know, Bobby? Do you

know anyone who has tried doing everything he wants to do?"

Bobby held up the magazine. "Why, Mother, this man in the magazine can do all that. It says so right here."

Mother took the magazine. "This is a beautiful house and a lovely garden and a fine car and boat the man has. But when I read the article, I did not find that it said the man had everything he wanted or could do anything he wanted to do. Or even that the man had a good time and was happy."

They looked at her, their faces puzzled. "But why wouldn't the man be happy with all these nice things?" Bobby asked.

"Perhaps he is happy, Bobby. But if he is, it is not because he has so much money and so many things."

"I don't understand why not," Bobby persisted.

"We all need some money and some things to keep us fed and clothed and healthy, son. But beyond that, being happy and

having a good life are different from having a great many things.''

"How are they different, Mother? I'd like to know.''

Mother smiled. "Sometimes having too many things keeps people from being happy, instead of making them happy.''

"Do they really? Do we know anybody like that?'' John asked.

"Jesus met a man like that one time,'' Mother told them. "A very rich young man came to talk with him. Jesus knew who the young man was and was glad to talk with him. 'I keep all the religious customs and laws,' the young man told Jesus. 'Yet I am missing something that makes life good. What do I still lack? What should I do to be what God wants me to be?'

"As Jesus looked at the young man he knew what was keeping him from feeling joyous and satisfied with life.''

"What was it, Mother?''

"The young man was thinking too much about all his possessions—his houses and lands and jewels—and how to keep them safe. They were on his mind, worrying him even when he was thinking about being close to God and helping people."

John pointed to the pictures. "This man might have that trouble. He needed a guard to take care of his fine things."

"Did Jesus tell the man who came to see him what to do about all the things he had?" Susan wanted to know.

"Jesus suggested a hard remedy, Susan. 'All those possessions are in your way,' he told the young man. 'Sell them and give the money to people who need it.' "

"But the man wouldn't want to do that," John protested. "You said he liked his possessions."

"That was just the trouble, John. He paid too much attention

to them. They were a burden to him instead of a pleasure."

Bobby puzzled over it. "Did Jesus tell the man what to do after he had sold all those things?"

"Jesus felt drawn to this young man, Bobby. He was strong and alert. Jesus wanted him to be the fine person he could be. To have a full life. 'Come with me,' Jesus invited. 'Come and learn what makes life joyous and good.'"

"Did the young man go with Jesus?" Susan asked.

Mother shook her head. "Though his possessions were not making him happy, he loved them too much to give them up."

John closed the magazine. "What happened to him?"

"His story has a sad ending," Mother told them. "This is the way it reads, 'He went away sorrowfully.'"

"That is a sad ending," Bobby agreed. "He didn't enjoy his possessions and he wasn't a friend of Jesus, either."

"I'm sorry for him," Susan added. "He lost all around."

"Jesus was sorry too, Susan," Mother said. "But the man put the wrong things first."

"Why wouldn't he let Jesus show him?" Bobby wondered out loud. Then he looked at the magazine. "Do you suppose we would do what the young man did? If we had to choose, would we choose all these things instead of being a helper of Jesus?"

"What do you think about it, Bobby?"

Bobby was quiet a moment. "I would like these things," he admitted. He sighed. "Why can't we do both, Mother? Have lots of nice things and care about other people, too?"

"Maybe we can, son. Nice things aren't *bad!* What Jesus was showing us is that if we let our possessions become more important than everything else, we will miss what is best in life."

"That's what the rich young man did," Susan said. "He missed being a friend of Jesus."

# Jesus Was Different

BOBBY'S room at school had been learning about music. A special teacher had come to play some records for them and to tell them about the music.

The boys and girls liked especially a stirring piece played by an orchestra. The teacher told them about the man who had written the music. About his exciting life, how hard he had worked, and how he had played before kings and emperors and popes.

"He lived a long time ago," the teacher said, "but his music is played today in almost all the nations of the world. He was a really great musician. We say he was a genius."

After they had listened to the work of the great musician, the teacher showed the boys and girls some musical instruments used in the orchestra and demonstrated how they were played.

"Could I try the little horn?" Bobby asked.

So several of the boys and girls had fun trying the instruments.

Bobby's daddy was passing near the school at closing time, so he waited to pick up Susan and John and Bobby. Bobby told him about the great musician's work they had just heard.

"What made that man a great musician?" John asked.

"You are beyond me there, John," Daddy said. "Many things, I am sure, go into the making of a musician."

"It is the same with artists and scientists and even football players, isn't it?" John persisted. "Some are great and some are just pretty good. I wonder why."

Daddy agreed. "There are many special gifts. Someone comes along who is far beyond the rest. We say he is a genius. But I doubt that anyone knows exactly what makes a genius."

"The teacher called that musician a genius," John recalled.

Susan leaned forward in the back seat. "Are all geniuses equally important? In what they do, I mean?"

"Some gifts seem more important for other people, Susan. And some geniuses use their gifts more generously."

Bobby had been thinking. "We have been talking about Jesus, Daddy. Was Jesus a genius?"

Daddy slowed the car to turn a corner. "He had gifts that no one else has ever had, son."

"How was he a genius?" John wanted to know.

"In a special way, John. He could enter into God's love more completely and share God's purpose more fully."

"To understand God was a very special gift," Susan said.

Daddy went on. "Jesus could also enter into the experiences of other persons more than anyone else ever could. He knew how they felt when they suffered and when they were joyous."

"Those gifts are more important than a musician's or a scientist's or anybody's, aren't they, Daddy? God gave them to Jesus, didn't he?"

"I think all our gifts are from God, Bobby. But you are right that Jesus' gifts were most important to everybody, everywhere."

"Jesus was generous with them, too," Susan added. "He didn't just feel close to God himself. He helped others feel it."

Bobby nodded. "And he didn't just feel proud about knowing what people needed. He understood how to help them."

"I think that Jesus was more than just another sort of genius among all the other geniuses," Daddy told them. "We say he was unique." He smiled as he explained, "That means the only one. There has never been anyone like him."

"Then how can we understand him?" John asked. "Since he was so different?"

"Well, we don't understand all about how the musician writes his music," Bobby reminded them. "But we know it is good."

They had reached their street and Daddy stopped the car.

"We know Jesus helps us feel close to God," Bobby added as he opened the car door. "That is what is important."

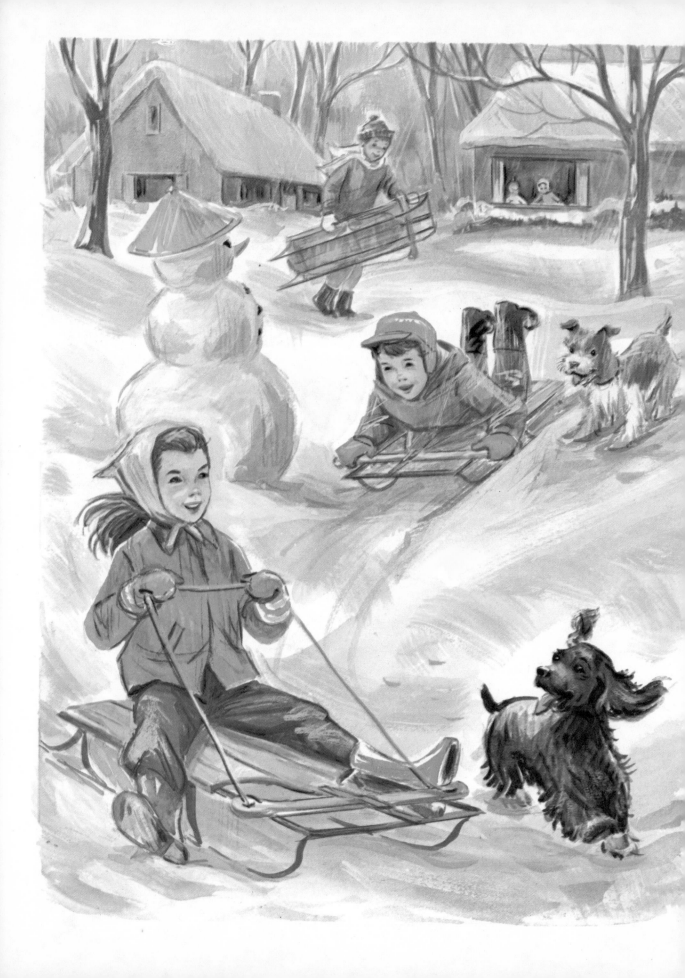

# Jesus Suffered for Others

BOBBY and Mary and their next-door neighbors had had fun building a snowman in their yard.

When Mary and Jack grew tired and had gone indoors, Bobby, Susan, and John went sledding.

It snowed all night. By morning everything was covered.

Bobby and his mother stood at the window. "Snow is fun," Bobby said, "but this is too much. I feel bottled up."

Daddy joined them. "That is what we are, son. Our radio had a message asking everybody to stay indoors."

Bobby turned on the TV. The announcer was talking about the pictures of the deep snow. Then another voice broke in. "There has been an accident. We switch you to the scene."

Listening, they learned a child was lost in the snow.

The TV pictures showed men hurrying into the dangerous, swirling white storm—stumbling, falling, struggling on.

Watching anxiously, Bobby and Mother and Daddy heard a shout. "We've found him! Bring shovels!" Soon they saw the

child, wrapped in blankets, being carried into a house.

Bobby breathed his relief. "That was hard, dangerous work. Those men might have been hurt. They were brave."

"They were good neighbors, Bobby," Daddy said. "I doubt they thought about being brave. They thought about the child."

Bobby turned off the TV. "Is that how to be brave? To think of what needs to be done? But not about yourself?"

"That helps, I think. There are many ways of being brave, you know. Some of them are harder than risking an accident to get a child out of a heavy snow drift."

"What kinds of being brave are harder, Daddy?"

"I think it is often harder for someone to stand up for what is right when other people are against him."

Bobby remembered what his group had been talking about at church. "Jesus was brave like that." He thought a minute and went on. "But what I can't understand is why those men turned against Jesus. He cared about people and helped everybody who needed him."

"One reason, I think, son, was because Jesus showed them God wanted them to care about everybody, too, and to help everyone in need. These men loved the people who agreed with them, their own friends. Jesus showed them this was not enough."

"They didn't like it? Being told they were wrong?"

Daddy nodded. "It made them angry to be criticized."

He continued. "Those men didn't like what Jesus showed them about God, either. They thought God cared for them more than for others because they followed the set rules and observed all the religious ceremonies. Jesus told them plainly that they had missed the main point. That God cares more about how men treat persons than about observing ceremonies."

Bobby thought about it. "Why didn't Jesus just let these men alone? And help those who wanted to listen?"

"Those who were angry with Jesus thought *they* were the ones who knew about God and his way for men," Daddy explained, "and that Jesus didn't. So they tried to stop him from teaching the people."

"Why didn't the people Jesus had helped back him up?"

Mother walked to the couch. "When all these important

men turned against Jesus, the others became afraid, Bobby."

Daddy sat in the armchair. "Some other men turned against Jesus for a different reason. They were disappointed in him because he had not organized an army to free their country from the Romans."

Bobby was surprised. "But Jesus was not a general. Why did these men think he would lead an army?"

"Because that was what they *wanted* him to do, son. They wanted a national leader or a king like David of old to fight enemies and make their nation again a great nation."

Bobby wondered about it. "They didn't understand Jesus, did they, Daddy? What he wanted to do?"

"Not at all, Bobby. But because they talked about a national leader, Jesus was accused of stirring up a revolt against Rome.

This charge made the Roman governor listen to those men who wanted to stop Jesus. Jesus was arrested by the soldiers."

Bobby was troubled. "Jesus helped so many people. Didn't anybody stand up for him and say what he was really like?"

Daddy shook his head. "Even his closest friends ran away and hid. Jesus was left alone."

"Alone with the enemy soldiers," Bobby remembered.

"The soldiers took him to Pilate, the Roman judge. Jesus was accused of plotting to be the country's king. Pilate condemned him. The soldiers took him away to be crucified."

"Why didn't God stop them?" Bobby demanded. "He should have stopped them from hurting Jesus like that."

"Should he, son? It is hard for us to understand why Jesus had to suffer. But I think Jesus understood."

"How did he?"

"We have talked about how Jesus showed by his life among men that God understands what it is like to be a human being in all his experiences."

Bobby nodded. "Like Jesus growing up and being hungry and working and standing up for the ones other men hurt?"

"All that and more, Bobby. Suffering is part of life, too."

"I don't like to think of Jesus suffering," Bobby said.

"But he did suffer, son. Because he suffered, we know he understood it and can help people who suffer."

"Go on, Daddy."

"But Jesus' suffering was more than that. He shared God's love for people."

"Yes, he did love people."

"Jesus knew that only love great enough to suffer for what people had done could show them how much God loves them."

"Did Jesus love those people?"

"Because men would not respond to God's love they sinned. Jesus suffered for them. But he did not stop loving them."

"How could Jesus love men who made him suffer, Daddy?"

"That is the wonder of it, Bobby. The wonder of the love of God which Jesus showed to men. It stopped at nothing. Jesus did not try to strike back at those who hurt him. Instead he prayed for them, 'Father, forgive them.'"

Bobby was quiet for a moment. "Jesus must have loved people more than anybody else ever did."

"He showed people the love of God, dear," Mother assured him. "He loved them not because they deserved love, but because it was his nature to love people—even when they were making him suffer."

"That was special love," Bobby decided. "Love for people who were hurting him."

"It is what we call redeeming love," Daddy explained.

"I don't understand it very well," Bobby said.

"None of us can understand it, Bobby," Daddy told him. "But people all around the world who have responded to Jesus have felt this redeeming love of God in their own lives."

"Have they, Daddy? What happens when they do?"

"They are like new persons, son. Because they know how much God loves them, they can love other persons, even the ones who are not lovable. They see life as it was meant to be. And they know it is good."

# A Promise Kept

IT WAS Easter Sunday. Bobby's church was beautiful with flowers. The choir had sung triumphantly, "Alleluia! Alleluia! Jesus Christ is Lord!" Walking home, Bobby was thoughtful.

"I need to understand more about Easter," he said.

"Do you, son?" his mother asked. "I think we feel special joy at Easter because it reminds us of Jesus' promise to his friends."

"The soldiers killed him. What promise made people glad?"

Daddy took Mother's arm and held Mary's hand as they crossed the street and Bobby walked behind them. On the other side, Daddy stepped back to walk with Bobby.

"Let's talk about Easter," Bobby said.

"You remember Jesus told his friends he was going to suffer," Daddy began. "That he was going to be put to death."

"But that was something sad. Not anything to be glad about."

"Jesus' promise was about something else he knew, son. He knew that the love of God could never die. The love of God filled his own life. He had shown it to people day after day as he lived among them. He would go on showing God's love to people."

"But how could he when he had died?"

"His body had been cruelly abused and buried. But Jesus' promise to his friends was that this was not to be the end of it all. The promise was that he would come again to them."

"Did they believe him? When they knew he had died?"

"At first they were frightened and hid in a secret place."

"Then how did they know Jesus kept his promise?"

"Because he *was* with them, Bobby."

"Was he, Daddy? Really with them after he had died?"

"They had no doubt about it, son. Even while they were hiding in fear. He was with them, close to them, comforting them, understanding them, forgiving them."

"The disciples believed his promise, then?"

"They knew it was the most dependable promise ever made. They understood that all things had not been made perfect. But they knew Jesus would be with them always."

"That made a difference, didn't it?"

"It made all the difference, Bobby. The disciples were not afraid anymore. They became new men."

"I am glad they stopped being afraid. What happened after that?"

"The disciples knew they would not see Jesus anymore as they had seen him. He would not be walking with them about the countryside teaching the people and helping all who needed him. Now Jesus depended on them to show people what he had shown them of God's love for them and God's way for men. He had said to them, 'Teach men all that I have shown you.'"

Bobby was still wondering, his face puzzled. "They knew Jesus was with them when they could not see him?"

Daddy smiled. "Jesus was not like a ghost to them, son. Nor an invisible companion such as Mary sometimes imagines."

"No, that would not be real," Bobby agreed.

"And Jesus was real to them. Real to their whole selves, their minds and hearts and bodies."

"Did the disciples do what Jesus trusted them to do?"

"Theirs is a wonderful story, Bobby. Men who had been terrified cowards now went out before the people, speaking fearlessly of all Jesus had been and done. They stood boldly before the same men who had sent Jesus to the Romans to be crucified."

"Nobody stopped them? When they spoke up for Jesus?"

"Some men tried. But the disciples were so joyous and so sure of what they had experienced that as the crowds of people listened, they, too, knew that Jesus was with them. They, too, felt his love and his power to change their lives."

Bobby thought about it all. "And we have Easter to remind us of Jesus' promise? That even being put to death couldn't stop him? That he was still with his disciples?"

"Not only with his disciples, Bobby. The love of Jesus who lived and helped people and suffered and died long ago is with us, too. He is the living Christ. God with us, and with people everywhere. Today as in the days of the disciples. And always."

"It is a big thought," Bobby said. "But I see why Easter makes people glad. To remember Jesus isn't just for long ago. He is for today, showing us God is with us now."